YOUR MAN

AN OWNER'S MANUAL

BY MARTIN BAXENDALE

..... right
Mr. Wrong
Mr. Tall-Dark-And-Handsome
Mr. Short-Fat-And-Bald
Mr. Perfect
Mr. Average
Mr. Wierdo
Mr. God's-Gift-To-Women
Mr. Farty-Little-Wimp
Mr. Sad-Bastard
Mr. New-Man
Mr. Toy-Boy
Etc...

© Copyright 1997 Martin Baxendale
Published by Silent But Deadly Publications,
21 Bisley Road, Stroud, Glos., England

All rights reserved. No part of this book may be reproduced, recorded or transmitted in any form without the prior permission of the publisher

ISBN 0 9522032 6 X

Printed in the UK by Stoate & Bishop Printers Ltd, Cheltenham, Glos.

INTRODUCTION

We guarantee that you will find your male unit such an amazingly useful and surprisingly handy gadget to have around the house, such a stunningly successful money-making device absolutely guaranteed (some day) to boost your household income to truly astronomical levels of luxurious living, and so much fun to play around with in the bedroom, providing countless hours (or at least countless minutes) of exciting and exhilarating personal entertainment, that you'll wonder how you ever managed without one.

SMALL PRINT: Please note, however, that in order to avoid prosecution under the Trade Descriptions Act we must point out that words such as 'useful', 'successful' and 'exciting' as used in the above product description and/or elsewhere in this owner's manual may not neccessarily apply to all available male units. You may find that some or even all of these descriptions are not in fact basic built-in features of your particular male unit model. (And as for that last bit, don't be in too much of a hurry about chucking your vibrator in the dustbin).

UNPACKING YOUR MALE UNIT

WARNING! Take care when unpacking your male unit. Due to in-built leakage problems and other revolting design faults unique to the male unit, inexperienced female owners and operators may find removal of the packaging a hazardous and traumatic task.

Indeed, we never recommend saving the packing materials in which a male unit first arrives in your home, for obvious health and sanitation reasons. Do not attempt to wash and/or re-use these packaging materials. Burn them, then open all doors and windows wide, and order bulk delivery of assorted room-freshner sprays, deodorants, anti-perspirants and biological stain-digesting washing powders. You'll need them!

RECOMMENDED SAFETY EQUIPMENT:

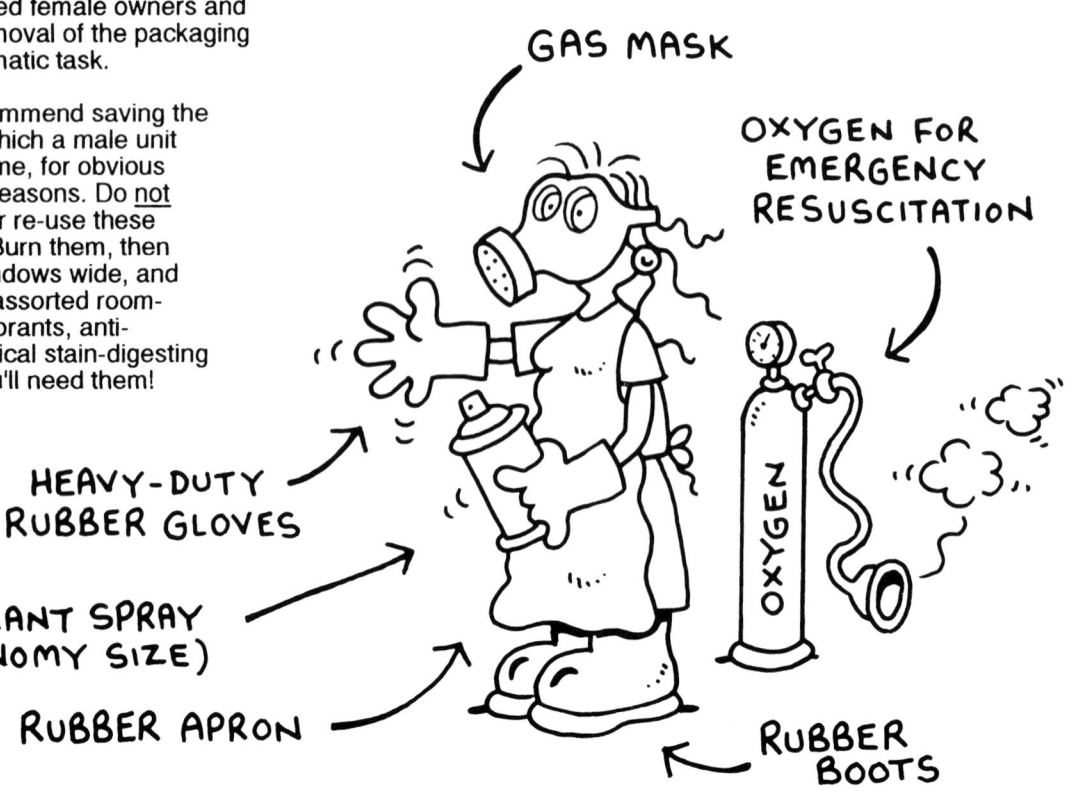

- GAS MASK
- OXYGEN FOR EMERGENCY RESUSCITATION
- HEAVY-DUTY RUBBER GLOVES
- DEODORANT SPRAY (ECONOMY SIZE)
- RUBBER APRON
- RUBBER BOOTS

TAKE GREAT CARE WHEN UNPACKING A MALE UNIT.
BEWARE HAZARDOUS PACKAGING MATERIALS:

- REVOLTINGLY STINKY T-SHIRT ARMPITS
- DISGUSTINGLY STAINED AND SKID-MARKED UNDERPANTS
- DECOMPOSING OLD TRAINERS
- OPTIONAL GREASE-STAINED AND DANDRUFF-FILLED CAP
- BEER-SOAKED AND/OR CURRY-STAINED T-SHIRT
- SICK-MAKING SNOTTY HANKIE
- OVERPOWERINGLY PONGY SOCKS

GETTING STARTED

NOTE: When unpacking and getting started with a new male unit, take care to ensure that these attachments are completely removed before starting-up, or at least very soon after you get going with your new unit. Continued running with these attachments still in place may seriously invalidate any guarantee of a long-term happy relationship with your male unit:

A) Ex girlfriend(s)

B) Ex wife/wives

C) Ex boyfriend/husband (if your new male unit turns out to be a sex-changed model)

D) Other previous romantic/sexual attachments involving, for example, domestic pets, farm animals, vast collection of pornographic material, etc.

BAAAA!

POWER SUPPLY

The average male unit's preferred power supply is roughly as follows:

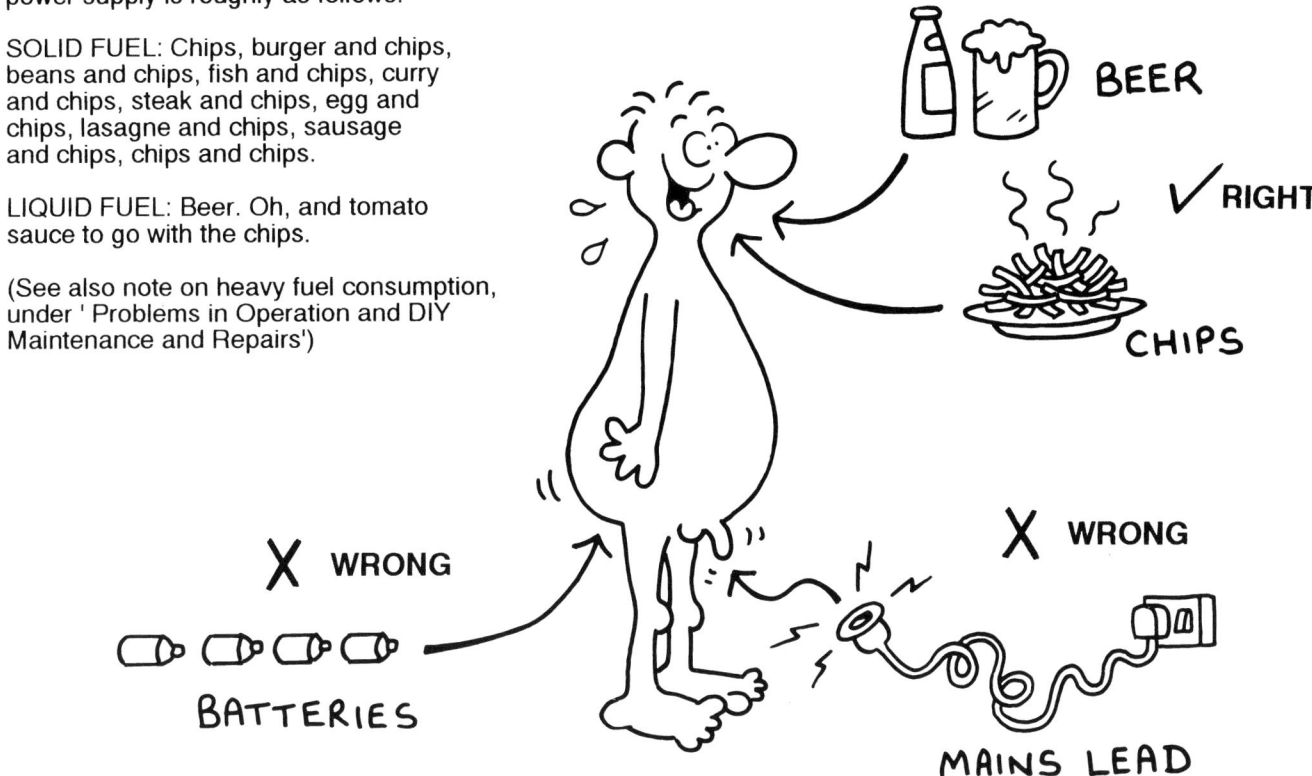

SOLID FUEL: Chips, burger and chips, beans and chips, fish and chips, curry and chips, steak and chips, egg and chips, lasagne and chips, sausage and chips, chips and chips.

LIQUID FUEL: Beer. Oh, and tomato sauce to go with the chips.

(See also note on heavy fuel consumption, under ' Problems in Operation and DIY Maintenance and Repairs')

BEER

✓ RIGHT

CHIPS

✗ WRONG

BATTERIES

✗ WRONG

MAINS LEAD

BASIC FEATURES

If you've never owned a male unit before, you'll soon become familiar with the unit's basic features. More experienced owner/operators will know only too well what to expect.

- BALD SPOT
- DANDRUFF
- NIFFY ARMPITS
- SCRATCHY FACE-SCOURING STUBBLE
- BEER/FAG BREATH
- SEXY HAIRY CHEST
- WOBBLY BEER-BELLY
- BREWER'S DROOP
- KNOBBLY KNEES
- FARTY BUM
- PONGY FEET

PARP!

BASIC CONTROLS

One of the first things you need to know about your male unit is how to get him to do what you want.

Of course, you could always try talking to him and telling him, but due to a major programming error male units seem to be incapable of actually listening to female owner/operators. Sorry.

Luckily the average male unit is essentially a very simple device, quite easily controlled even by the most inexperienced of female operators. The basic means of control include (not necessarily in the following order):

A) Crying B) Having sex C) Not having sex D) Nagging E) Sobbing F) Sulking G) Still not having sex H) Punching, kicking, scratching and biting I) Throwing things (preferably his things) J) Threatening never to have sex ever again K) Having sex L) Walking out M) Solicitors N) More solicitors

NORMAL OPERATING POSITIONS

Your male unit has various operating positions, but those illustrated here are the ones that you'll come across most frequently:

POSITION NO. 1

Used for:

Helping-With-The-Housework Mode
Putting-Up-Shelves Mode
Looking-For-A-Job Mode

POSITION NO. 2

Used for:

Decorating-The-Spare-Room Mode
Mowing-The-Lawn Mode
Talking/Listening-To-Female-Owner Mode

POSITION NO. 3

Used for:

Helping-Put-The-Kids-To-Bed Mode
Doing-The-Washing-Up Mode
Walking-The-Dog Mode
Just-Coming-Up-To-Bed-In-A-Minute Mode

OPERATING POSITIONS IN SEX MODE:

(A) 0 → 3 MINUTES:

(B) 3 MINUTES → NEXT MORNING:

(C) FOREPLAY POSITION: See Position No. 3, Coming-Up-To-Bed-In-A-Minute Mode.

OPERATING MODES AND FUNCTIONS

ONE-NIGHT-STAND MODE

If on your first encounter with your carefully selected and long-awaited male unit you start to suspect that he may be operating in One-Night-Stand Mode, while you had planned a much longer-term relationship, then we strongly recommend the following simple procedure:

A) Get male unit stinking drunk

B) Take male unit to tattoo parlour and get them to tattoo the following on his chest, back, arms, buttocks and genitals:

Your name, address and telephone number, fax number, E-mail address, and date, time and place of Registry Office booking, plus a number of strategically placed tattoo pictures of yourself in various erotically arousing nude poses.

C) Wait for him to call

NOTE: With an existing male unit, this procedure is equally useful for security-marking purposes, to help deter other female operatives from trying to nick your male unit (especially if he's prone to slipping into One-Night-Stand Mode when you're not around to keep him under control).

SEX MODE

There are all kinds of exciting and stimulating games you can try out with your male unit once you've got him into Sex Mode.

It's not difficult getting most male units going in Sex Mode. One flick of the joy-stick and they're off. More often the problem is keeping him going. There's nothing so frustrating as finding the GAME OVER signal flashing before you get your go, and having to constantly remind your male unit that these are supposed to be two-player games.

WHIP

DRIP-FEED FILLED WITH HIGH-ENERGY GLUCOSE & VITAMIN SPORTS DRINK

CRACK!

THREE-MINUTE EGG TIMER MAY SHAME MALE UNIT INTO MORE PROLONGED PERFORMANCE THAN USUAL

ZAP!

ELECTRIC CATTLE-PROD

SPURS CAN BE HIGHLY EFFECTIVE BUT HARD ON THE SHEETS (AND NOT RECOMMENDED FOR WATER-BEDS)

JINGLE!

KEEPING YOUR MALE UNIT GOING IN SEX MODE

NIPPING-DOWN-THE-PUB MODE

Many male unit owner/operators find this an extremely annoying operating feature as it tends to click-in at the slightest excuse and constantly over-rides other more useful modes; such as Doing-The-Washing-Up Mode, Helping-Put-The-Kids-To-Bed Mode, Putting-Up-Shelves Mode, Mowing-The-Lawn Mode, Painting-The-Spare-Room Mode, and Talking-To-Female-Owner Mode.

HOW TO INITIATE: Nipping-Down-The-Pub-For-A-Quick-Pint Mode can easily be initiated by any of the following events, but especially by all three occurring in quick succession:

A) Dinner finished

B) Nothing on TV

C) Front Door Left Open

HOW TO CANCEL: There is no guarantee that any one of the following measures on its own will cancel or prevent operation of Nipping-Down-The-Pub Mode. However, trying all of them together might just possibly delay it for a night or two:

A) Lock, bar and bolt all doors, windows and sky-lights (<u>and</u> don't <u>forget</u> the <u>cat-flap</u>)

B) Hide Wallet

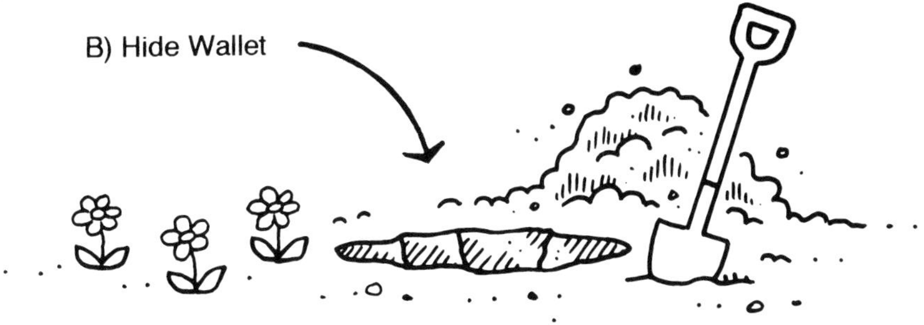

C) Try to initiate Sex Mode

D) Physical restraint (handcuff and tie to chair)

BOOB-OGLING MODE

This is a basic operating feature of most male units but has not become a favourite with female owner/operators, who tend to find it extremely irritating.

Unfortunately, it has proven difficult or even impossible to re-programme male units who regularly display this highly embarrassing mode. However, it's always worth a try, and we would recommend the following procedures more or less in the order that they are listed:

A) Sharp elbow-jab in ribs

B) Clip round ear with handbag

C) Pint of beer tipped over head

D) Knee in groin

E) Ask local riding stable to fit a set of blinkers

If none of these procedures prevent repeated operation of Boob-Ogling Mode, then we strongly recommend that you trade-in your male unit for a new model as soon as possible.

PUTTING-TOILET-SEAT-BACK-DOWN MODE

This is one particular operational function which our engineers have spent countless days and years trying to programme into the average male unit, with virtually no success at all.

You're welcome to try your hand at re-programming and de-bugging your particular male unit's basic operating parameters to include this functional ability, but you're probably wasting your time. Their grasp of the very concept seems to be about as vague as their aim is when operating in Standing-Up-And-Peeing Mode.

The only thing we can suggest is that you fit a strong spring to your toilet seat, to ensure that it snaps firmly back down on its own when released after your male unit has finished peeing.

EDUCATIONAL MODES

Your male unit has various educational functions and modes guaranteed to broaden the horizons and widen the knowledge of the whole family.

A) Helping to increase your children's vocabulary

DADDY SAID "F***ING HELL" AGAIN!

B) Helping you to improve your driving skills

...INDICATOR.. MIRROR... TOO CLOSE TO THE CAR IN FRONT.. OVERTAKE.. ..SLOW DOWN.. BRAKE!!

OH SHUT UP!

IF YOU'D JUST SHUT UP AND LISTEN FOR ONCE, YOU MIGHT **LEARN** SOMETHING!

C) Teaching you just how bloody annoying the average male unit really can be

USEFUL EARLY-MORNING WAKE-UP FUNCTION

Arguably a useful feature if your alarm clock is on the blink, but not always the most welcome male unit function so early in the day.

NOT SO USEFUL MIDDLE-OF-THE-NIGHT WAKE-UP FUNCTION

This operates in various ways, as demonstrated here:

CHANGE-JANGLING FUNCTION

A highly entertaining function displayed by most male units at some time or another, and apparently a major repetitive operating feature of some models.

Liable to cut-in at any odd moment that your male unit is otherwise comparatively immobile and inactive (e.g. standing in pub bar, waiting at bus stop, standing in queues, or hanging around impatiently while female owner/operator shops for clothes/shoes or chats to friend in the street).

BALLS-JUGGLING/POCKET BILLIARDS FUNCTION:

Very similar to Change-Jangling Function. Less noisy, but potentially much more embarrassing when repeatedly performed in public.

CONNECTION TO OTHER DOMESTIC APPLIANCES

Nice idea. Shame it won't work. Our engineers aren't sure exactly why, but it seems that the average male unit is completely incompatible with most domestic cleaning appliances, and especially those to be found in the kitchen and/or utility room areas.

So, while the idea of trying to get your male unit connected to and working with other household machinery is obviously very appealing, in practice you will most likely find that he is totally incapable of correctly operating such complex domestic cleaning hardware as washing machines, tumble driers, vacuum cleaners, kitchen sink taps, and toilet brushes.

I'LL NEVER FIT ALL THIS WASHING IN THAT TINY DRAWER!

PROBLEMS IN OPERATION AND DIY MAINTENANCE AND REPAIRS

Unfortunately, the average male unit suffers from so many basic design faults and programming errors that, to be perfectly honest, you're likely to have nothing but problems with him. Sorry.

FART!

GAS MASK

CATALYTIC EXHAUST + SILENCER

EXCESSIVELY NOISY AND SMELLY EXHAUST PROBLEMS

This is one of the commonest complaints from female owner/operators about the day-to-day operation of their male unit.

Various ways of coping with the problem have been tried, but the only real long-term answer is to convert your male unit to cleaner, less polluting fuel.

CONVERTING YOUR MALE UNIT TO CLEANER, LESS POLLUTING FUEL:

✗ WRONG — BAKED BEANS

✗ WRONG — CURRY

✓ RIGHT — SALAD

✗ WRONG — BEER

✓ RIGHT — FRUIT JUICE

HEAVY FUEL CONSUMPTION

Excessive fuel consumption and/or regular intake of extremely high-octane fuels can lead to unacceptable levels of weight-gain in your male unit, posing serious health risks to his continued operational viability.

And on a more technical level: All that revolting wibbly-wobbly flab....sexual turn-off or what?!!!

There are basically two possible ways to correct this problem. Good luck!

A) INITIATE <u>EXERCISE MODE</u>: Not easy. Often, especially with some older male units, bloody impossible. Still, you have to try.

To initiate Exercise Mode, strip male unit naked, stand in front of full-length mirror, point at reflection and laugh hysterically while waving pin-up picture of Tom Cruise in the nude.

Essential equipment: Running shoes, sweat-shirt, paramedic resuscitation team.

B) **CONVERT YOUR MALE UNIT TO LOWER-OCTANE FUELS:** And you thought option (A) was difficult!!

✗ WRONG - HIGH-OCTANE FUELS:

BURGER & FRIES

HOT DOG

FAMILY PACK

CRISPS

BEER

✓ RIGHT - LOW-OCTANE FUELS:

SALAD

FRUIT JUICE

NOTE: You may find it easier to convert your male unit to healthier, lower-octane fuels <u>gradually</u>. For example, starting him on something like Chips and Bean-sprouts before moving on to pure salads.

SMOKE AND FUME PROBLEMS

Many female owner/operators of male units worry about their unit constantly smoking during daily operation. And with good reason.

If your male unit is allowed to continue smoking over a prolonged period, and especially if smoking is heavy and non-stop, then this can have a serious effect on the unit's general efficiency and overall life-expectancy. And, just as important, who wants to kiss an ashtray (let alone shag one)?!

RECOMMENDED ACTION: Complain, nag, argue and plead; then remove all tobacco from vicinity of male unit and apply anti-smoking patches and/or gum on a daily basis until smoking problem is cured or male unit is reduced to a gibbering nervous wreck (but an <u>alive</u> gibbering nervous wreck).

ANTI-SMOKING REPAIRS:

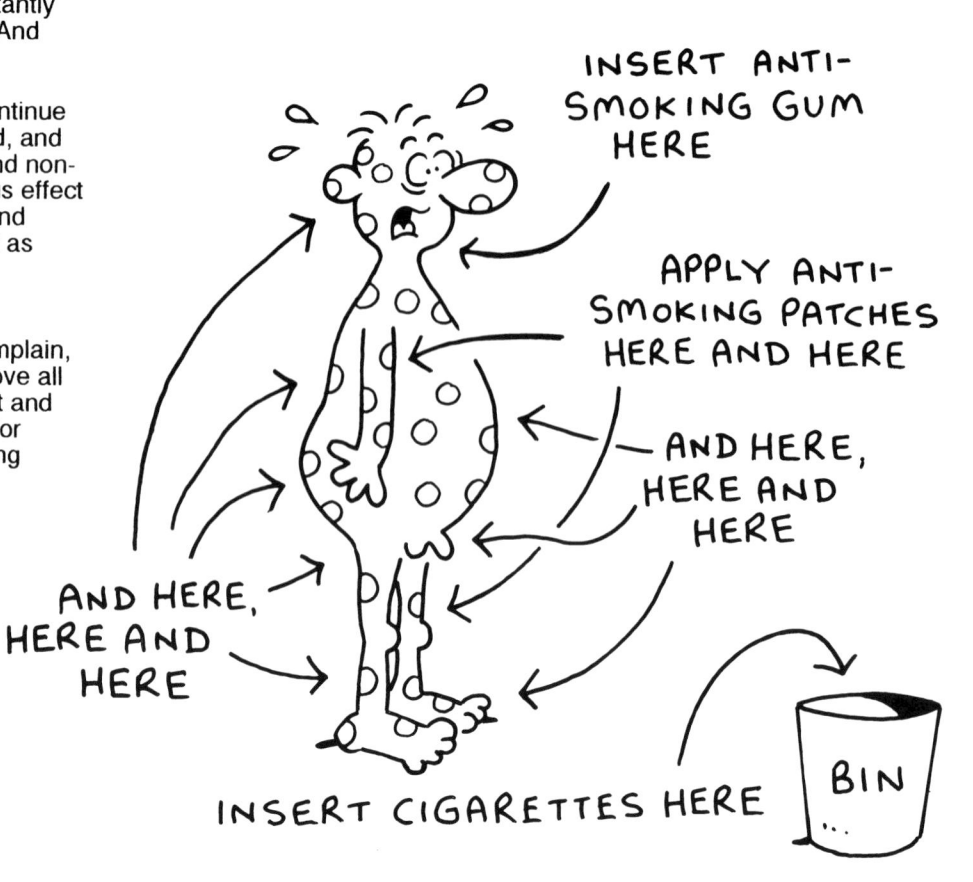

INSERT ANTI-SMOKING GUM HERE

APPLY ANTI-SMOKING PATCHES HERE AND HERE

AND HERE, HERE AND HERE

AND HERE, HERE AND HERE

INSERT CIGARETTES HERE

BIN

GETTING YOUR MALE UNIT STARTED

Some male units can be very difficult to get started first thing in the morning, especially in cold weather, so here are some simple tips on how to ensure that you always get your unit up and running on time.

ELECTRICAL INTERFERENCE

Despite the utmost care during design and manufacture to ensure that all male units meet both national and international electrical standards, we regret that your male unit may seriously interfere with your TV reception and VCR operation.

Having a male unit in your home will tend to restrict your TV reception and video viewing to sports programmes, 'bang-bang, you're dead' action films, soft porn, nostalgic re-runs of old kids' programmes, and anything starring Demi Moore, Arnold Schwarzeneger or baby-eating zombie alien creatures from outer space.

GOAL! GOAL!! BANG! BANG! EAT LEAD, PUNK! OH YES! GIVE IT TO ME, BIG BOY!!

UP-GRADING YOUR MALE UNIT

There are numerous optional add-on extras that can be fitted to your male unit to up-grade and improve his performance in various operating modes:

BATTERY-OPERATED TONGUE EXTENSION: For improved Sex Mode performance.

VIBRATING BATTERY-OPERATED WILLY EXTENSION: With multiple-movement function and long-life batteries, for enhanced Sex Mode performance.

PROGRAMMING UP-GRADES: To enhance and expand your male unit's basic (usually very basic) Sex Mode.

BRAIN

EXTRA-LARGE EAR EXTENSIONS: So that, just maybe, he might actually listen to you occasionally.

WARNING! UNAUTHORISED ATTACHMENT:

BIT-ON-THE-SIDE: If found to be attached to your male unit, remove immediately. Failure to do so may invalidate any guarantee of a happy long-term relationship with your male unit.

TRADING-IN YOUR MALE UNIT

There are many different types of male unit (see list of available models, page 1) and eventually you may well find that you are tempted to trade-in your old unit for a new, improved high-performance one.

But beware. Many male units may claim to be top-of-the-range, executive-style, go-fast, do-it-all MR. PERFECT models. However, apart from a few minor differences in styling and appearance, most male units are actually pretty much the same basic bog-standard unit underneath.

What's more, due to the wide range of design faults and programming errors that seem common to male units of all types, most models are equally likely to fail to live up to promised or expected performance levels. So don't be taken in by the sales talk.

You may find the following model notes especially useful when making your trading-in choice.

TOY-BOY MODEL: This male unit <u>play station</u> is designed for exciting, fast-moving games-playing, ideal for more experienced female owner/operators who have already mastered and grown bored with the more basic everyday work-station type of male unit

Exciting games you can play with your Toy-Boy model male unit include:

✷ ZAP THE BULGING BOXER-SHORTS.

✷ SLOW DOWN, WE'VE GOT ALL NIGHT.

✷ WHAT? AGAIN? <u>ALREADY</u>?!!!

'NEW MAN' MODEL: Helps with the housework, looks after kids, talks to you, listens to you, cuddles and hugs, etc, etc

Contrary to widespread advertising and publicity, this particular male unit model is <u>not</u> yet widely available.

The 'New Man' model was briefly believed to have been perfected and to have flooded the male unit market, massively out-selling all previous types. However, it has proved successful only as an experimental prototype. In daily use it has failed to operate to the high specifications set for it, and has been temporarily withdrawn. <u>Beware cheap immitations</u>.

31

EXTENDED WARRANTY

With regular care and attention, your male unit may well last you a lifetime.

For a one-off payment of just £50, the manufacturer can offer you a special <u>extended</u> <u>guarantee</u> that you will be blissfully reunited with your beloved male unit for all eternity in the after-life period following expiry of the basic lifetime warranty; together again for ever, and ever, and ever, and ever...

Alternatively, for a one-off payment of just <u>£100</u>, the manufacturer can guarantee that you <u>won't</u> <u>be</u>.